If This Gets Out

Tony Sims

If This Gets Out

Tony Sims

Paperback Edition First Published in Great Britain in 2015 by aSys Publishing

eBook Edition First Published in Great Britain in 2015 by aSys Publishing

Disclaimer

ISBN: 978-1-910757-34-5

aSys Publishing
http://www.asys-publishing.co.uk

Table of Contents

The Chair

He bought a book
   on how to do upholstery
purchased special hammers
   gimp pins, webbing
and working slowly
   as instructed
laid bare the dusty bowels
   of his father's chair

came to admire
   each crafty tuck and corner
noticed with a smile
   the odd mistake

saw virtues
   in what before
had seemed so baffling

came at last to understand
   why he had bought the book
and dared to touch the chair.

A Word

A word,
   simple, unattractive,
spurred by a moment,
   out of place perhaps,
but only slightly so,
   not wholly meant,
but nearly so,
   yet the wrong word,
no doubt of that,
   worse now spoken,
a mischievous word,
   booming its echo in us,
kindling angers,
   seized upon,
irrevocable,
   wreaking havoc
beyond syllable,
   a clenched word,
never whispered,
   and now with us,
until its power wanes . . .
   . . . if it ever will.

Words Of One Syllable

Strange that it should be so,
Be born and live and grow,
Watch weird new worlds go by
In the blink of an eye,

Wake up to days of gold,
And shake when nights grow cold,
Hear frogs plop in still ponds
Fringed by ranks of tall wands,

And quake as mad March mirth
Stirs seeds in the warmed earth
To shock a Spring, and spray
White may in a green May.

So with day's drum beat done,
When cool clouds hide the sun,
Twist an awed head to pry
At gems spilt in the sky.

Strange that it should be so—
This non stop ebb and flow,
Fixed in a flux of ghost
And flint and blood—yet most

Strange of all, though our din
Of brave words is lost in
A deaf wind's rise and fall—
The breath to say it all.

The Thought

The thought when it came
was good no-nonsense stuff
and in my waiting game
quite enough

reward for patience.
I turned it upside down
for proof of provenance,
judged weight, walked round,

viewed every angle.
No room for doubt—
a true original—
and mine throughout!

Then it started bouncing,
slowly at first,
followed by a flouncing
from side to side and worst

of all it started breeding,
groaning and cloning,
clamouring, stammering,
bugling, saxophoning

in a froth of fantasy
no tongue could utter—
pure feckless ecstasy.
Then in a flutter—

a sudden twinkling
wriggling shimmer,
trimmed to an inkling
and gone in a glimmer.

I Died Yesterday

I am six years old
a child of the bombed village. It is spring
and my father's field is still not planted.
We have had a hard time since he went away,
but mother says he will soon return
now the foreign soldiers have gone.
The planes have stopped coming
and it is quiet in the hills.
My brothers are rebuilding the house
while I play on a patch of earth,
chasing butterflies and talking to lizards.
Mother gets angry when I do this,
but I like to explore and feel the sun
on my back. Today I found something
buried in the soft earth,
and tried to dig it out. . .

I died yesterday .
    and I want to know why.

I am an old man,
with an old man's cunning -
always neutral in a war -
that's how you get old in my country.
My sons took sides and they're dead now.
I was crossing the road to the bakery
to fetch the fresh crisp loaves
my wife loves so much, picking my way
through the debris of last night's
bombardment, past the boy with the gun
in his usual position. He waved me by
with a smile—he might have been my grandson.
Then at sound of firing in the alley

the boy with the gun knelt
and sprayed shot into the shadows,
and into the sun. . .

I died yesterday
    and I want to know why.

I am a mother from the south, where the land is burnt
My husband is away fighting.
I have two young children now—one died
on the long march to get here.
We have been in the camp many months,
and our days are marked by hunger
and the pain of waiting. Some say
the food convoy has been attacked
and destroyed only a few miles from the camp.
I must try to stay alive to look after
my young ones. We are weak, too weak—
to ask questions. I keep my limp children
close to me. It is difficult sometimes
to tell day from night. There is a ringing
in my ears

I died yesterday
    and I want to know why.

I am a young man
with a pretty girlfriend.
We have been going together for about a year
and plan to get married next spring.
I am studying to be a doctor
so I know all the right precautions.
My younger brother left to join a group
in the mountains. One day last week
the soldiers came and took me to a barracks
where they beat me and questioned me.

They asked me questions I could not answer.
They wired me to my screaming -
they made me one with my screaming,
putting answers to my pain.
I told them all I thought they wanted to hear -
but it was not enough. . .

I died yesterday
   and I want to know why.

I am a middle aged man
with middle aged problems -
and two teenaged daughters. One of them
is getting married soon. I don't like him much
but she seems to know her own mind.
I have never been in any kind of trouble,
but once forgot to send in my tax return.
I was going down the road to post,
and some invitations. It was fairly dark .
And no one was about. Someone I could not see
called out a name. I was not my name,
so I went on. Again the name was called,
and I stopped. A man appeared in front of me
with a gun. He shouted the name again
and fired. . . . .

I died yesterday,
   and I want to know why.

Recrimination

My love and I live out our numbered days,
Pretending still that nothing is amiss,
While each of us in deftly chosen ways
Collude in our unspoken armistice.

I know the stratagems and secret smiles,
That camouflage an eagerness to go;
Am almost taken in by all the wiles
Intending me to think it is not so.

But I have learned a compensating guile,
And, stooping low, have come to recognise
Reflections of myself that I revile,
Unlikeable likenesses that I despise.

And though the coming pain I shall outlive,
The self disgust I never shall forgive.

The Difference

Being different, if only slightly different,
Might have made a difference, we liked to think,
Enough perhaps for both of us to sink
What differences we had, emerge more tolerant.

Luck might have helped us out to some extent
But luck needs humouring—a nod, a wink,
Some bait—so we have only ourselves to thank
For all the twists of our predicament.

And which of us can find the will to change,
That curbing of a niggling urge to blame,
Sufficient to defer, perhaps forestall
Our fate, to make our commonplaces strange,
But being the same, defiantly the same
Nothing now makes any difference at all.

Valediction

Don't walk away from me, at least not
Not while we still have moments to explore
The fringes of our pain, to talk and fret
Our petty troubles just a little more.

Don't talk away from me, for such restraint
Conceals a muted temper of unease,
So whisper now your loudness of complaint,
Leave judgment to the arbitrating trees.

For us, it seems, no logic can persuade,
No new-born strategies transform the game
That you and I so skilfully have played
Until the only consequence is blame.

And if you choose to go from me let's have no
Trifling gestures of regret, just go.

Seasonal Love

I had a springtime love once,
Blissful and sweet.

> Flowers smiled
> On my ecstasy.

We had a summer's madness,
Wanton and wild.

> Trees talked
> Of our lunacy.

In autumn came our quarrel,
Stormy and short.

> Leaves curled
> At my jealousy.

Winter saw our parting,
Sullen and dark.

> Gales swept
> Through my misery.

Now spring is here again,
Grinning and green.

> Flowers preen
> At their sorcery.

Free Time

Given scope to do what we would do,
Or say we would if left to our devices,
We take fright, prevaricate, submit to
Petty tyrannies, contrive excuses

For circumspect delay, invent imperatives
In stratagems of can't and must, with foolish
Foresight, and a grumpy knowingness that drives
Us to deny the here and now, to banish

Instant opportunities to distant dream.
And so we blemish calendars and diaries,
Ready to lattice all enfranchised time,
Leaving our wistful selves to haunt interstices,

Unruly temperaments eager to give in,
Pinioned by freedom, freed by discipline.

Pharisees

We all saw it, all of us who were there,
caught in a bubble of blue morning,
glinting in sunlight and swaying in the still air.
We saw how its huge arc of wing cast shadows
on the grassy slope, gazed in wonder
at its consummate form, noting each detail
of glittering plumage, and the head's proud curve,
as it swayed in that still air, the glare
of its omniscient eye bewitching us.
For a full minute it swayed and hovered,
then wheeled a wide circle,
soaring west to indigo mountains.
All of us felt the thrill of witness,
knowing as we stared at each other,
that we had been changed by what we had seen—
changed utterly.

Later in the day, when we returned
and told of our encounter, the smart sophists
and clever pharisees got down to work,
pooh-poohing our earnestness, eager to dispute
our testimony in sneering tones.
Impossible, they said, there were no precedents,
nothing in the records to support us.
These self-appointed guardians
of our common wisdom, were always on the look-out
for evidence to fit a dull consensus.
They argued that we were mistaken—a touch of the sun perhaps,
or a trick of light—common enough
in that thin mountain air.
We tried to reason with them, insisting
there were no dissenting voices amongst us,
that what we had seen in that bright sunlight

had been seen by us all. But these skilled catechisers,
practised in their doubting, these clever ones
who had not been there, were quick to dismiss us with a sneer,
to unsettle us and foster our bewilderment,
so that one by one our certainties vanished,
and what we had seen became a figment,
at first argued over, but in the end, embargoed.

And so what we had all seen, or thought we had seen,
crouched for a while in crannies of the mind,
but by evening, for most of us, had slipped away,
to reappear perhaps, on other sunny mornings,
when the air was still, soaring in from indigo mountains,
casting a shadow on other grassy slopes.

But for some of us the evening air was empty;
night left in a hurry and we woke early
wondering what another dawn would do
with its new-found day.

Numbers

Just two of us
    at first
making love
    in one to one communion
binding separate lives
    with hands held
to keep away the dark

then three

newcomer-noisy
    demanding
another kind of love
    a newer union

and redefining forever
    our sense of number.

Having

We have, and proving it need do no more
Than show to others what it is we have,
And intimate we have enough, or more
Than enough, for our needs; but when we have

So visibly enough, or more than enough,
What does it prove but that we need no more?
In any case is having enough enough?
Is there not room perhaps for something more?

Having nothing though is more than enough
To prove a need, for clearly not to have
Wants for no proof—is always plain enough
To catch the eye of those who have.

Have-nots have no need for special claims, enough
For them to be without, more than enough.

Soldier

He went away to a war
    made him tough and wily
put inches on his chest
    to hang a medal from
taught him cap-badge Latin
    potted regimental history
bizarre geographies
    of bar and brothel
drilled him in simple skills
    with bayonet and grenade

when fully trained
    unleashed him on a hillside
in the crump and panic of a battle
    among psalms of singing shrapnel
left him for dead
    blood ebbing from boots

came back and married sensibly
    a plain girl with a soft voice
who cooked like his mother
    and like his mother
kept a spotless house
    took a job as watchman
but fearful of silences
    changed to the clank of a dairy.

in time seeded parts of himself
    to tell his story to,
but didn't,
    bought a dog instead

grew tulips and forget-me-nots
   fat leeks and abundant beans
in a tidy garden
   where solitude ripened
where he sometimes started at a sudden sound
   or saw menace in a thrush.

Dream Garden

As day is forced open by long levers
Of light a wind waltzes the cherry trees
Scattering blossom in chill gray air,
And crooked paths condense from shadowed mist.
Here slumped over a low wall's edge aubrietia
Insinuates its silken strangleholds
And lines of spiny lupins start to sway
Like cobras, their agitated leaves hissing.

In borders gangs of warring primulas
Seek their revenge on panic stricken pansies,
While round the muscled oak installations
Of sinister daffodils are busy gathering
Intelligence for powers underground.
Disquieted now I tiptoe through minefields
Of unexploded bulbs, ignoring anxious
Crocuses, with mouths held up like hungry chicks.

Nearby, some gladioli, brilliant hilted
Excaliburs, lie scabbarded in soft soil,
And just beyond a regiment of smart
Tulips troop the colour past the sundial.

Newly awakened flowers stretch and swell,
Evidence that teams of gnarled gardeners
With birds-feet hands and game soup skins
Have been hard at work fattening their charges
On clever diets of dried blood and crushed bone -
Lethal Merlins, spreaders of toxic mist,
Anointers of deadly balm, stealthily
Perpetrating pogroms on slug and snail.

Accosted now by loitering peonies,
Camouflaged cabbages, who flaunt their blousy
Charms like street girls, I turn away,
And there, alone, besieged by her admirers,
The haughty rose, smiling her perfumed treachery
Behind a barbed entanglement of fangs.

And from a wall of glowing brick, a huge
Wisteria, decked in full medal display,
Hangs motionless, much like an anaconda
In fancy dress, watching over the ash
Of dead bonfires and wormy compost heaps,
Reminders that misfits and murdered weeds
Have rotted and smouldered here unprotested.

But images dwindle and on a curl
Of acrid smoke I am called to a calmer
Sleep by the trembling tolls of fuchsia bells.

Hollywood Upbringing

Shrugging his shoulders like Humphrey Bogart
he left my Hepburn mother at the door,
tears on her cheeks, tea towel in hand, watching his slow stride
into a technicolor sunset.

I could tell something was wrong the moment
he thrust a crumpled note into my hand,
muttering that I was now the man of the house.
My younger sister Shirley twigged it too,
and shaking her curls of barley sugar hair,
kicked me on the shin and started to cry.
Apart from a newspaper photo—
which mother did her best to keep from us -
we never saw him again.

When the letter came she burst into tears,
prowled around the house for hours on end,
straightening mirrors and rearranging things—
as distracted women seem to do in films.
After the evening meal she told us how father
had been involved in a dangerous mission abroad,
dying bravely in some kind of ambush.
She made it clear that we had to be specially proud of him—
though she never mentioned his name again.
For a long time we rummaged all her hideaways
but never did find the letter.

I got through my James Dean period
without too much trouble, endlessly practising his walk,
his talk, his repertoire of smiles, and how he spat.
Mind you I couldn't take this sort of thing too far
because my boss at the store was pretty strict.

Not that anybody seemed to notice—there was no one around
like Liz Taylor to look good and snigger at my jokes.
Some scripts you can't do anything with.

The lodger was put in the room next to me.
He was a crazy Walter Huston kind of character
who laughed a lot and made his own cigars.
When he wasn't practising the violin
he spent most of the time in the kitchen
playing crib with mother and filling the house with his smoke.
Mother would say, with an edge to her voice,
that he had been wounded in the war and planned
spending the rest of his life on light duties.

When mother got married to Walter Huston
Shirley refused to come to the wedding.
She had left home after a row about eye shadow,
had her hair cut short and dyed black. She drove around town with a
married man twice her age.
and turned out to be a real Bette Davis sort of bitch.

As for me I got used to a step-father
making me laugh with his tales of the war
and teaching me the odder facts of life.

But I still can't figure out
why my Bogart dad only had a bit part.

A Quiet Murder

It was a quiet murder
    as murders go.

The wedding went with a bang
    big marquee
lots of champagne -
    teeming trays
of multi-coloured canapes,

    but no photographer.

For the ceremony
    the victim's bride
wore subtle shades of puce
    and a daring hat.

The victim drank little
    standing apart
from his talkative new wife.

You could tell
    she had planned it all
from the beginning,
    down to the last detail-
taxi to the airport,
    two weeks in Portugal
flamboyant luggage,
    then back to a cosy flat
above the butcher's shop.

When it was all over
　　there was little to go on -
a missing person report, but
　　no body, no murder weapon,
nothing you could call a clue.
　　The police were baffled
and their file is still open.

Rumours were rife of course -
　　odd sightings, mutterings
of something not quite nice -
　　but no one now talks openly
and the victim was never seen
　　again in these parts.

Men In My Life

In the film last night,
   after a long fight,
Robert, the nice one,
   played it straight and won
the girl of his dreams.
   But for me, in his arms,
each passionate word
   that I overheard
was whispered to me
   on my comfy settee.
So I felt no shame
   when the moment came
for a blissfully tender
   complete surrender
to my dream lover.
   Nothing will ever
be like that again.

No wonder some men
are worshipped like gods.

I cried afterwards.

When Ken came back from darts,
   full of beer and farts,
he tripped on the mat,
   swore blue at the cat
and before our eyes met
   had switched off the set.
Then turning his back
   he wolfed down a snack
and without a word said
   he dragged me to bed,

where quickly undressed,
   except for his vest,
he fumbled my breasts,
   made half hearted thrusts,
got rapidly bored,
   turned over and snored.
Mum said married bliss
   would end up like this.

Men are such bastards.

I cried afterwards.

Rivers

Rivers know a thing or two, how to keep
Their heads down making the best of high ground,
Curled up in contours, smoothing pebbles round,
Scrawling signatures on unclaimed landscape.

Off to a good start they can't wait to skip
About, show off in mill race and fast weir,
Duck bridges, revel in flash floods, career
In full spate to the marker-post top.

But nothing lasts, their jaunty progress slows
To sidles through cities, as more and more,
Encumbered with wreckage, debris and silt,

They lose their way in a jigsaw of oxbows
Or dawdle on dirty mudflats before
Foundering in harsh waves, drowning in salt.

Happenings

Why doesn't something happen -
   as it did yesterday
and the day before?
   Even just now I could tell
something was about to happen,
   but it took fright, tiptoed away,
leaving me to think
   that when it does happen,
if it is going to happen,
   something indefinable
may intervene,
   to stop it happening here—
a happening next door perhaps,
   where something always seems to happen,
or make it happen here
   when I happen to be out, or,

what is worse,
stop anything happening ever again.

Prodigy

City celebrity, takeover prodigy,
Chairman at thirty three, nationwide company,
Famed for his industry, and generosity.

OK, but it doesn't fool me.

Flat in the Albany, villa in Tuscany,
Chateau in Burgundy, schlosses in Germany,
Manor near Newbury, big as an embassy.

So what—do you think he's happy?

Forested properties, horses with pedigree,
Wife's aristocracy, fine Norman ancestry,
Winsome and willowy, crusted with jewellery.

Simple enough—money and snobbery

Bronzed masculinity, classical symmetry,
Sculpted so cunningly, and so appealingly,
Like some divinity from Greek mythology.

Self-publicity cuts no ice with me.

Brilliant family, talented progeny,
Innate ability, born to supremacy,
Sporting and scholarly, all at the Varsity.

Pure silver spoonery.

Hugo and Gregory, law and accountancy,
Fleur and Penelope, Greek and philosophy,
Children of destiny, prides of the dynasty.

Darlings of unequal opportunity.

Mistress in Bloomsbury, popsy in Camberley,
Chambered in luxury, pampered like Royalty.
Talk of debauchery—prompted by jealousy?

    Never satisfied if you ask me.

Bounteous to charity, champions ecology,
Environmentally green as a laurel tree,
Gifted linguistically, reads Chinese poetry.

    Can afford to can't he?

Swills beer heroically, sips claret critically,
Skilled anecdotally, excellent company,
Plays cricket locally, loved universally.

    There' has to be a flaw—has to be.

Wooed by society, prized by the peasantry,
Lives life so utterly bloody ecstatically
It's indescribably way beyond equity.

    And that, in a nutshell, really does floor me.

Voice Of Authority

I'll tell you what truth is, confided Pilate,
And somehow we could tell he wasn't jesting,
Quite plain to those who care to make the effort -
Not much to do with beauty or anything

Like that, nor matching argument to fact,
But something simple to get hold of, yet so
Beneficial in overall effect
It's all on earth you ever need to know.

The truth you see is what I say it is,
No more, and though some awkward dissidents
Kick up a fuss and want it otherwise
They soon come round to good old common sense

So spellbound are they by the symmetries
Of half-truths and the sorcery of lies.

Alibi

Where were you when the oil was spilled
And the whales and birds and fish were killed?

Taking tea in a tasteful spa.
Witness says you went by car.

Bye bye alibi
Bye bye.

Where were you when the forests burned
And the jungle floor was charred and churned?

Sat at my window free from blame.
Witness says it's a hardwood frame.

Bye bye alibi
Bye bye.

Where were you when the hot core blew
And the fields were smeared with poisoned dew?

Reading far into the night.
Witness says by electric light.

Bye bye alibi,
Bye by

Where were you when the ice caps thawed,
And oceans over the lowlands poured?

Sunning by my parasol.
Witness saw an aerosol.

Bye by alibi,
Bye bye.

Where will you be when the world goes sane
And the rhinos romp on the plains again?

Up in front and shouting loud.
Witness has you in a shroud.

Bye bye alibi,
Bye bye.

Tiny Feet

They called it knowledge
    passed it on down the centuries
letting it seep from culture to culture—
    wise men adding to it
from time to time.

They invented ways of storing it
    on clay, parchment and paper
filled books with it
    created vast libraries
as playgrounds for scholars.

And with it came power
    it's growth seemed unstoppable -
convincing proof
    of a privileged place
under the sun.

No one spotted the flaw,
    no reckoning was made
of pitiless contingencies.

And after the mass extinctions
    only insects survived
coming to rule the planet
    as natural conquerors.

Having no use for knowledge
    they gnawed the libraries

    . . . and multiplied..

Bigamist

The girl in his head
   ran away to hide
from the impish grin
   of the girl in his groin
who was out to spoil
   with withering spite
all the girls in his eye
   and the blundering brides
who burdened his bed.

Wall Mender

The drystone wall divides the sheep-strewn hill
like a parting, and climbs for a furlong
to the horizon before it arches
out of sight into a further valley fold.
Old Ben, bandy as a bicycle clip,
crouches by the wall, his weather beaten cap
crowning a head much beaten by the weathers.
Behind him on the grass lies an old army
small pack with sandwiches of thick corned beef,
and lavish slices of brown doorstep bread,
(carved in the dawn-cold kitchen
of his clammy cottage), two chocolate bars,
a peeping thermos of strong sweet tea,
and a neatly folded tabloid to provide
helpings of bosom and catastrophe
for wry consumption in his lonely breaks.
His bicycle which he has pushed a mile
from the nearest road, leans against the wall.
Sturdy and without gleam, its battle scars
are mantled with a dull and mellowing rust.
In front of him one of several breaches
in the wall, a consequence of intruding
bramble, subversive frost, or a simple lack of will
to hold together—a place that tall spindly grasses
and vagrant leaves have made their own.

On one side are piled creamy coloured
pieces of freshly quarried stone,
sharp edged as broken crockery. On the other
a smaller heap of weathered mossy stones
taken from the wall itself, while in between

a rough assortment of rubble and shards
that somehow will be used to wedge and pack
the reconstructed wall. Old Ben has cleared
away the plants and debris to reveal
the jagged edge of the gap. Selecting
a piece of stone he tries it at the base.
of the breach. Not satisfied he searches
for another, larger stone, a process
unhurried and deliberate. The stone
now chosen is neatly put in place;
then more, until the whole base course is laid;
and then another course, longer this time,
each stone sloping forward to discourage
any welcome to insinuating rain,
each placement a seeming necessity.
Sometimes he takes a fragment in his hand
to trim a corner or remove a lump
with a ringing tap of his sharp stone axe

In the pub at night, behind a slow-sipped pint
of bitter beer, Old Ben discounts the skill
by saying simply its just a matter
of one stone on another—nothing more.
And yet his listeners seek a mystery,
and deaf to simple explanations discern
a fellowship of cunning hand and brain,
some deeply rooted wisdom that springs
from the soil itself.

Pausing and stretching every now and then,
not to involve himself with earth or sky,
or to witness sudden tremors on the grass.
He spares no time to notice flowers
except that they are white or pink or blue,
nor birds, except their endless chattering.

His temperament is suited to the pace
of lonely tasks that give him time to wander
lightly through his store of memories:
a wife long dead, and children gone away;
of wartime friends (for him a happy time),
the hardships of a disappointing peace,
rewards not striven for and not deserved,
wrongs not righted, efforts not repaid.

The horizontal stones have all been laid,
and make a rough-darned patch of new and old.
Placing the last upright header stone
Old Ben stands back, looking neither pleased
nor proud. He turns and sizes up
the remaining gaps in the wall. 'About
a fortnight, ' he thought, 'til Whitsun'
and gathering his things he prepares to move.

Persona

As a new day begins
its shenanigans
shall I put on gray
to keep it at bay

a discreet brown
disguising the clown
that wriggles inside
or let fate decide?

As matters of weight
seek to infiltrate
with relentless prod
I solemnly nod

keep a straight face
my hidden grimace
wrinkling the skin
of a demon within.

While nubile newscasters
detail disasters
I only think
they're better in pink.

My manner is grave
but my thoughts misbehave
and can find no room
for planetary doom.

So when the skies redden
over Armageddon
I shall be found
on the merry-go-round.

Where is the sense
in this dissidence -
how pigeonhole
such rigmarole?

And how long go on
acting Solomon
while inside cool
thinking the fool?

Weapon of Mass Destruction

Perfect weapon, ordained for death and distance
Bold in concept, brilliant in execution,
The boast of generals, plaything of statesman
And tyrant, an engineered magnificence,
Sculpted masterpiece of strength and elegance,
Empowered by uncanny navigation
To menace oceans, pinpoint bunkers, bludgeon
Cities to debris and blood at a glance.

Yet able to wake on an April morning
From the rubble of sleep with a bright tingle
In the blood, play wry monarch or fool, sense
Infinities in a wild mind's imagining,
Be moved close to tears by anthem or jingle
And sometimes to weep over death and distance.

Wonders

Not brochure-fresh Marrakesh
or broken biscuit pyramids,
no sponsored trips to Gilgamesh,
or trudging past the caryatids.

No visits planned to Disneyland,
or rickshaw rides round Singagpore,
no camel trains to Samarkand,
or tiger shoots in Bangalore,

nor yet to see the Taj Mahal
or Venice by the Grand Canal.

But happy here, in enthralling
routine, with nowhere to go
but out, and about, with nothing
to do, today or tomorrow,
but eye with rapture
the footloose regiments of ants
manoeuvring on dirt, or capture
the commonplace in a dance
of awesome insignificance.

Armchair Statesman

Not for him the courtesies of conference,
Or tiptoed diplomatic compromise;
No cautious balancing of arguments,
Frustrated by the irksome exercise

Of poring over documents and maps,
Revising boundaries again and again
As fragile talks face danger of collapse,
And weaponry is cocked to guide the pen.

His way the insoluble is curt,
No-nonsense, ever ready, with superb aplomb,
To marshal boundless forces, to subvert
By blackmail, terror, massacre and bomb—

For to his artless repertoires belong
Only means that are simple, deadly and wrong.

Halfway House

Nothing begins, for where are beginnings
To begin, and how decide the change
From what was not to something new, how rearrange
And punctuate the flux of things with endings?

Likewise nothing ends, for when we talk of coming
To an end all boundaries blur to strange
Uncertainties and vagueness at the fringe
That makes of every end a form of middling.

So should we then in our uncertain love
Loiter at ease behind the lines, or struggle
To find coordinates in no-man's land?

Better enjoy the presents that we have
And leave untidy time to sort its muddle
Before our middling lives begin to end.

Lament For Mr Nobody

The government spokesman set out to make it absolutely clear, absolutely clear.
Mr Nobody, in his heart of hearts, knew that it was nowhere near.

Nobody could spell it out for Mr Nobody.

The newspaper baron had made a pile from the gutter press, from the gutter press.
Mr Nobody found daily papers a distasteful mess.

Nobody could interest Mr Nobody.

The High Court Judge addressed a crucial legal point that was arcane, that was arcane.
To Mr Nobody it was only all too plain.

Nobody could fool Mr Nobody.

The Chancellor rose to tell the Chamber of his fears, of his fears.
Mr Nobody's whelk stall friends had known all this for years.

Nobody could convince Mr Nobody.

The Honourable Member worked the system hard for his preferment, for his preferment.
Mr Nobody only wished for his interment.

Nobody could hoodwink Mr Nobody.

The Noble Lord had paid a tidy sum for his ennoblement, for his ennoblement.
Mr Nobody had no time for ermine or for Parliament.

Nobody could impress Mr Nobody.

The barrister knew his guilty client would go free, would go free.
Mr Nobody was wrongly charged with a minor crime but made no plea.

Nobody could fathom Mr Nobody.

The banker took his bonus with a smile, and bought another mansion, another mansion.
Mr Nobody had mortgage trouble and feared a repossession.

And nobody could soothe Mr Nobody.

The Prime Minister decided to start another war, another war.
Mr Nobody's soldier son was sent out on another tour.

Nobody could explain to Mr Nobody.

The union boss called his members out on strike, out on strike.
Mr Nobody had lost his job and was already on his bike.

Nobody gave a job to Mr Nobody.

The Minister of Health declared he had the answer, had the answer.
Mr Nobody's wife was in the wrong post code and died of cancer.

Nobody felt the loss like Mr Nobody.

The Chief Constable hailed the drop in violent crime as a turnaround, a turnaround.
Mr Nobody, when walking home one night, was beaten to the ground.

Nobody came to the aid of Mr Nobody.

The Home Secretary announced a crackdown on illegal immigration, illegal immigration
Mr Nobody whose daughter had been gang-raped by asylum seekers, showed no elation.

Nobody could pacify Mr Nobody.

The Bishop spoke to an empty church on the need to forgive, need to forgive.

But Mr Nobody could not forgive, and had lost all will to live.

Mr Nobody trudged to the edge of the nearest cliff, and jumped.

And nobody mourned for Mr Nobody.

The Georgian

A nonentity -that's how they thought of him
At the seminary, always a quiet one,
A bit remote, but not a man to shun -
Poor student perhaps, but no real harm.

The party welcomed him, gave him a home,
Harnessed his cunning and application,
Rewarded his loyalty to coming men,
Hailed his deference to the leader's whim.

In time, himself a man of steel, scalpel
Sharp, whose rivals fled, or simply ceased
To be, whose loaded pen shrank the peasantry,
Slithering upward, unperturbed by scruple,
At last becoming what all had least
Expected and most had cause to fear—an entity!

Visitation

He came, as usual, unannounced, all smiles
And handshakes, breathless with apology:
'Just passing, thought I'd call', glib denials
Of bother merely quickened cordiality.

'Come in, we're glad to see you, kettle's on'.
'Can't stay for long, tight schedule I'm afraid'.
An ad hoc meal proposed was seized upon
With all the charm that practice can parade,

And later, after all the asking-after,
An offered bed, three times refused, an evening
Of disappearing scotch and measured laughter,
A night disturbed by bathroom blundering,

He left, with strict instructions, so he said
To call on bosom friends in Sanderstead.

Along The Road

Along the road
a man
his wife
and daughter
in single file
not looking
to left
or to right
not speaking

hatless
in hot sun
going where
this man
his wife
and daughter
in the heat
along the road.

Road Death

A splotch of blood and tissue
badges the country road.
Was it a frantic rabbit
in a final feckless scurry,
some brazen pheasant
strutting out of place,
or an acrobatic squirrel
leaping elastically the wrong way?

It doesn't matter now,
for all that remains,
formless and unnameable,
paints a presentiment
stark against the tar.

Man At The Door

Man at the door
Angry, knocking
Face at the window
Pallid staring
Plane in the sky
Silver droning
Girls in the garden
Neatly playing
Bird on the pole
Rigid watching
Wife in the bed
Listening listening
Youth at the curtain
Peering peering
Boys on the turf
Batting, bowling
Cat on the wall
waiting stalking
Thief on the stair
Stealthy, sweating.
Girl with the pram
yawning yawning
Babe in the cot . . .
Crying crying
Old man dozing
Slowly dying
Son at his side
Silent waiting

Neighbours

In the universe next door
they move to different melodies,
gliding through colonnades
and courtyards bright with sunlit fountains,
forever partly hidden by screens
of fantastic tracery.

When they come among us
we know them by the set of the head
and cryptic camber of the smile.
Their women, wearing strange tiaras,
and necklaces of heavy gold, shimmer
as they walk in garments of the finest silk.
When early sun strikes the windows
of their tapestried chambers
devoted slave girls hasten to anoint
them with priceless attars.

We cannot plumb the logic of their laughter,
or their quarrels—sudden bursts of anger
followed by uneasy calm—nor the silence
which attends their solemn feasting.

When the year's fate is in the balance
they gather in homage to an unknown solstice
and, led by their holy men in crimson robes,
surround a secret altar of carved chalcedony,
lustrous with sapphires, and stained
with patterns of sacrificial blood.
When their chanting ceases we know
that rites with blade and fire
will be performed

We watch them, fearful
That one day they will notice us.

No Laughing Matter

As the joke puffed its way to an orgasm
we swayed with our beer, preparing explosions
of practised mirth to punctuate our sadness.
The ritual over, Jim began his tale,
based, he kept repeating, on real events,
and memorable because he never seems aware
he's told it to us many times before.

My joke turned out a moderate success.

Then Jake, whose brand of cryptic smut is culled
from sources he refuses to disclose,
told us the one about a group of monks
trapped in a lift at the Eiffel Tower,
which no one got—we chuckled anyhow.
someone even managing a raucous boom.
When it was Alan's turn to buy a round
he muttered, true to form, something about
his wife being ill and smartly slipped away -
which made a useful break for stretching legs
buying more beer, mocking Alan's meanness
and his repertoire of unfunny jokes.

An aura of knowing concupiscence
was the highlight of George's contribution -
a complicated story about a team
of randy gymnasts at the Commonwealth Games -
chock a block with anatomical detail -
which kept us all guessing right to the end,
and earned a burst of boisterous guffaws.
But Quentin, stoked up now with several whiskey
chasers, pretended not to get the point
by asking silly questions, so that George,

who takes his humour very much to heart
got so incensed he threw a glass of beer
in Quentin's face, and stripping off his coat,
loosening his tie, started squaring up
in a convulsion of bare knuckle rage.

He prowled about a bit, but when he threw
a vicious punch, we had to sit him down,
while a nervous Quentin tried to make his peace.
The landlord had by this time called the police;
the bar had cleared except for those who stayed
to witness how the pantomime might end.
An ugly woman drinking Baby Cham
grimly announced that we should be ashamed -
grown men in suits, behaving just like louts -
And so we were, but Eric had to make
things worse by calling her a stupid bitch -
which started up a further peevish row.

It was peaceful when the constables arrived.
Quentin had dried his shirt and George gone home.
A spirit of penitence filled the bar.
Nobody thought it funny at the time
But now when I think of it I have to smile

We go to a different pub now,
still drinking too much and telling the same old jokes.

The Gardener's Tale

Nice drop of rain last night,
Nice for the grass that is
Nice day now though

Nice garden this
Nice people to work for
Nice big house
In a nice part of town
Nice big statue by the entrance
Nice touch that.

He's nice enough when you get to know him
Nice wife
Nice manner she has
Nice with the milkman
Nice way with the cleaning woman
Nice with anybody really
A really nice woman.

Nice kids
Nicely brought up
From a nice home you see
Nice little private school up the road
But it pays off because they teach them nice manners.

He seems to be doing nicely enough
Nice car, goes with the job
Nice position in the firm too
Doing very nicely he is.
Must take home a nice tidy sum
Especially after that nice little windfall last month
Nice bit tucked away I shouldn't wonder.

They tell me he's got a nice office on the top floor

All nicely done out, all modern.
Nice big mahogany desk and swivel chair.
Nice secretary
A really nice looking girl.

Nicely spoken, a bit of real class,
Some say a nice bit on the side,
Which is not a nice thing to say
But still, there's talk of nice goings on after lunch
Nice bottles of wine in the cabinet
Nice little afternoon get togethers
Sometimes a nice hotel afterwards
Or is it a nice motel
Anyway somewhere nicely tucked away from it all
Nice little set up.

Nice that is until
His nice little foot in it
Nice how d'you do then
Nice big bust up
Nice bit of ranting
Nice kids screaming all over the place
Nice big bruise on wife's face
Sounds of nice home being broken up.

Nice big care reversing
Down nice big drive
Into nice big statue
Nice bit of tearaway driving
Sounds of nice big crash up the road,

Quite nasty really.

Bogman

In the beaded bog
he lies, chin to rim,
amid a swirling
spawn of vomit.

Sepulchre-still
he seems swollen
in the deep river
of his anguish,

The dark fetid
swamp of his mouth,
a place of elvers
and livid tongue,

caked with fenland
mud, slavering
the succulent moss
of his moustache.

His speckled nose,
like a squashed toad,
plays inert host
to a tiptoed fly.

Who now can scorn
this drooping foetus?
Who dares approach
such monumental pain?

I saw him first
in the public bar,
later the saloon,
in greedy swallow,

his wicked blackberry
eye reflecting
tawdry splendours
in a smokey gloom.

His frail fingers,
whitened to the bone,
gripped like tendrils
each swaying glass.

Stern omen now
of all that might befall,
each circumstance
skewered to memory.

Pitiful supplicant
in a closet ritual
of prayer or blessing
forgiveness or curse.

Bookworm

Alone in bed, stroking her cat,
she read the great love stories
of the world, pausing at times
to entice into her mind
the man at the bus-stop
who always smiled, and who once
gently held her arm to prevent a fall—

only to dismiss him
with the hauteur of an empress,
and return to the true passions
pressed within pages.

Boots

They had marched all day
　　under tall skies
from who knows where or why.

left right, left right
　　boots on concrete,
boots on tar.

by the river and through the park
　　marching along, humming a song
sniffing the evening air.

left right, left right
　　boots on gravel
boots on grass.

marking time at the barracks gate
　　through the arch, across the square
company strength, marching in threes.

left right, left right.
　　boots on cobbles,
boots on flags.

into the building single file,
　　pounding the corridor, still in step,
into the barrack room, straight ahead.

left right, left right.
　　boots on floorboards,
boots on tiles.

heading now for the outside door
　　then suddenly gone in a crack of light
with only the sound of marching beyond.

Left right, left right, left right.

Drinking Man

Bathed, shaved, and aftershaved
as if for a new mistress,
he rummages in a tiny wardrobe
for his last unstained silk tie,
selects, with apparent care, his only jacket,
pulls on his drinking boots,
(lately splashed, but wiped over),
and putting a finishing touch
to his once elegant moustache,
stands splendidly to attention
in front of the mirror,
ready to face anything,
except perhaps himself.
On his way out he gestures
to his knowing landlady
that he will not be late,
and strides to the usual bar.

What will it be tonight?
A couple of pints to start with
and whiskey chasers? Or some
chromatic cocktail just for fun?
Choosing was what he liked to call
his little drinking problem.

The bar is empty.
this bit he likes best -
time to scan a photograph or two
of a frail woman and two sad children
in a ragged garden. Time to muse
on the compensations of a lonely life
and reflect, with occasional clarity,

on a self trapped in dungeons,
resigned, but stoically sober,
slowly drinking himself to death.

He goes to the bar and orders
his first large scotch.

Planter

He commanded his garden like a regiment,
Inspected daily faultless rows of beans,
Reviewed with pride his ranks of well-drilled seedlings
Revelling too in blossom's peaceful pageant.

His wife got used to restless winters spent
In thumbing catalogues while he made plans
For spring offensives, long summer campaigns,
Hankering, as ever, to live in a tent.

But when this gentle soldier of the soil
Grew too weak to trim the hedge or discipline
Unruly climbers she was there to save
The glories of their flowered citadel.
And when he died she saw him well dug in,
And placed a single tulip on his grave.

Shoot To Kill

The first bullet
scored the chest
a second, heart targeted,
met instant success,
felling the awkward bulk
of crumpling carcass
empty-handed to the dirt,
blood spurts already
medalling the shirt.

Moving closer
gun held steady,
point blank
at the unaccusing stare,
trigger finger ready
to make a point
again and again and again,
all misgivings gone
as scores were settled
one by one by one

And later,
gun handed in,
armourer's tally taken,
rounds accounted for,
a brief debrief
and short report,
went home
to a talkative wife
and a daughter
swotting for exams.

Out

I am not in
despite sly digs
and mutterings
to the contrary
I am not here

and never was -
at least for long.
I'm always away,
or about to go away,
or having just come back,
packing up
to go away again.

That's why
it's so difficult
to catch me in.

But when
I'm somewhere else
a part of me always stays
to keep an eye on things
just in case.

When I'm away though,
sizing up elsewheres,
panning for gold
in dirty cities,
betting on certainties
and losing my shirt,
getting into the hottest water
or pouring cold
on sizzling suns,

When I'm up to no good
boozing and brawling,
talking out of place,
paying dear
for a warring tongue,
looking for love
in unlikely places,
passing the stare
of sullen strangers,
with a black dog
snarling at my heels,

my fate is always
to wake unawakened,
permanently stunned
by a breathless stupor
somehow neither here
nor there.

So if you find me out
don't be surprised.
Make yourself at home.
And if you have to go
before I get back
no need to leave a message -
I'll know you called.

Transaction in Normandy

A wet Normandy road leads to cloudscapes
of claret poured on apricots. We stop
for petrol by a ramshackle pump,
the numbers auburned by seeping rust.

Honeysuckle clusters everywhere.

He trudges through rainbow puddles,
pursued by female anger, his huge rubber boots
rumbling on broken tarmac. His mumbled replies,
brave but unheard, match unseen gestures of defiance.

Clanging pans, moved with needless clamour,
descant the scolding.
Garlic mingles with honeysuckle.

He grasps the nozzle with a hand
wise to the innards of engines,
the dark slop of their moving parts,
and tipping the peak of his cap
allows a smile to cross the rhubarb speckle
of his face.

Combien m'sieur?
Le plein s'il vous plait.
We struggle through a phrasebrook
chinwag on the imminence of rain.
He nods at my drowsy passenger:

Madame est fatiguee.

The hidden tympanist opens a window.

Replacing the nozzle he shrugs.

I pay, he counts, we part,
each smiling at our differences.

Essence of petrol, garlic honeysuckle everywhere.

Monster

When the dust had settled
after the latest explosions
some kind of normal life was restored,
and it was then they offered him a leading role.

We want you to be the monster, they said,
for a monster he had been,
in life and in fantasy,
a fitting choice for such a part.

You must be padded out
to show a monster's girth,
your face moulded to ape a monster's grin.
You must study the monster's gait
his leer, his frown, his stupid smile,
become proficient in the whole repertoire
of monstrousness.

When you lope onto the stage
we want you to make us laugh,
and yet make us afraid,
When evil flows from your smile
we want to tremble and feel safe.

A full supporting cast will be provided:
the good guy, a little smug perhaps,
but with some telling lines;
a sacrificial virgin with nothing much to say;
a poet-leader keen to legislate
for the soul of the nation;
and resplendent bishops to bless the guns,
a cocky general, lean and literate,
with his fat corporals lolling in the food trucks,
dishevelled guards at checkpoints

twirling cigarettes with trigger-weary fingers
—and of course a crowd of starving extras.

None of these will be a match for you.
You will be the star.
You must play it for all you are worth
so that when the stage is bare
we'll know there's a monster in the wings.

We want to mock you and fear you,
watch with fascination your wicked ways
and at the end delight in your destruction.
We know of course there is no cause for comfort:
the swotted fly always bloodies the wallpaper,
the trodden beetle curses as we crunch.
Grief never is enough to sweep away our guilt,
or anger loud enough to make the damage good.
We can only look, and cry and hope,
and pray for turning points.

Till then what else can soothe the pain
but entertainment?

That's why you must be our monster, they said.
This you must do for us.

Men Of The World

Who are all these funny people
with funny walks and funny looks
talking funny too, though never to me
—only to others with equally funny expressions
—or to microphones.

When they get off the plane
they seem quite used to carpet
on concrete, stiff smiles
of welcome, raised swords and ranks
of glistening soldiers.

One of them made a joke just now -
and everybody laughed—the way they do
at commonplaces in uncommon places.

This one has a draft agreement
in his pocket, put together by underlings,
that one, a signature up his sleeve -
waiting for the conjured moment.
He speaks to the middle distance
about his recent address to the United Nations
on how to save the planet.

It's all very odd, and I try to tell myself
that they know what they're doing.
Left to me I'd get angry
and the world would fall apart.

Somebody has to do it though.
I'm glad it's not me.

Where would we be without
such men of the world.

Rulers

What is left when the rulers who rule
by consent of the ruled argue that real
progress to the dream is beyond our reach,
for the moment at least, that too much
of of a good thing is bad, that we must
tighten our belts, do our uttermost
to understand that wise government
is not simply a matter of giveaways,
that more deserts stretch before the next oasis,
that the ever-fanciful excesses
of the shadow promisers are bound to lose
touch with reality, and bring about our doom -
while those rulers in waiting seek democratic
blessing for change in the name of freedom
of choice—what can be left to the unbelievers
who know that our so-called freedom of choice never
gives us the choice to be free of either.

The Sorcerer

Deep in our forest lives a sorcerer
who devours woodcutters for breakfast,
and is very partial to pretty girls
on duty visits to their grandmothers.
Schooled in the arts of alchemy he is able
to distil an essence of the purest venom
from the simple spirits of good will -
so giving him a fearful hold on us.

Some rumour-mongers said that he had perished
in the great battle between the white knights
and the black knights, when righteousness prevailed
and the splendid banner of our white king
was set in triumph on the city walls,
but it now seems he managed to escape
in a hay cart dressed as a man of God.

Now from a forested lair he seeks revenge
by exercising his stupendous skills,
concocting vile sherbets and toxic sprays
to poison our wells and pollute our clouds,
breeding huge locusts to destroy our crops
and gnaw the vital timbers of our homes.
His spies are everywhere; secret groups
of followers are plotting day and night
for his imminent entry to the city.
Our weak-kneed government has taken fright:
a hundred maidens have been offered,
prayers said in all our churches, and seven goats
sacrificed each day in our public squares.

But nothing seems to curb his plans for conquest -
the time for spineless gestures is past -
we must destroy him before it is too late -

we must burn our mighty forest to the ground!

Word Processing

Put it into words
   or even one word
seek and sift
   soliloquise
modulating
   word against thought
thought against word
   contrapuntally
each changing each
   until capture
or partial entrapment
   puts words, or a word,
to it . . .
   . . . or nearly it.

Uncertainty

Here happy I
   under April sky
content to lie
   with half-closed eye
on ecstatic high

There happy she
   in the shade of a tree
content to be
   exclusively
ecstasied by me?

Ends Of The Earth

He left the stench of collapsing cities
and trekked to the ends of the earth
to see what happened there.
When nothing did he laboured back
to middle ground, set up camp
on a dismal plain,
and knew that God had not remembered him.

He drilled below the deepest shale
deeper and deeper to the molten core.
He watched the gaudy turmoil,
shrank from the peeling heat,
knowing that God, if he had remembered,
did not care.

Was there a clue, he wondered
in the nearby sky,
beneath the planetary vapours
embedded in patterns of kaleidoscopic ice,
or beyond in the nebulous void
so empty he felt that God
had fled to another cosmos.

So he asked no further questions
and filled his days with the day-to-day,
sought a sheltered valley
and built a house of stone.
He found love a perfect antidote to doubt,
made gardens in the flinty soil,
fathered three thundering sons,
and a daughter more knowing than Cleopatra.
He filled his house with fruit and flower,
and sang a twilight in his pillared hall,
knowing now, that God, if he did exist,
no longer mattered.

Funeral

Important to be seen, and see, to be here,
In black tie and dark suit, noting absences
Of friends and some surprising presences -
Study the multi-coloured windows, and falter
In half forgotten hymns that others
Render heartily, ponder the expectancies
Of this place, its murmurs and silences
At arrival of hearse or wedding car.

Important to think of him as he was -
How his beliefs, or those he spoke about,
Never brought him here on Sunday, and how enticed
By love of earth and fear of fire, he chose
To rest in crowded ground with the devout,
Laid as he prescribed with his feet pointing west.

Falling Apart

I heard a bomb go off the other night.
Not a big bomb, I thought, in the circumstances -
little more than a reminder really -
but could it be the start?

My busybody neighbour heard it too,
said it cracked the plaster in his hall,
frightened the parrot and set his wife
to whimpering. Next morning, very early,
there were movements in the square,
and not by locals either. But he wasn't bothered -
so he said.

On my way back from work tonight I passed
a bed on the pavement, perfectly made up,
with stiff white sheets and brilliant patterned quilt.
Passers-by quickened pace, affecting unconcern,
while I, waving to a non-existent friend,
crossed to the other side.

Then at the corner by the coffee shop
I heard another bomb—about a mile
away it seemed—but still too close for comfort.
People stopped, many saluting the empty sky,
while a soap-box evangelist
gazed seraphically up as if
his point had been confirmed.

There was nothing on the news about the bombs-
Government policy I surmised -
but there's no disputing something is afoot.
Three more explosions in the hour after midnight,
by my count, and that last one was very close.
It shook the crockery—and wasn't that
the sound of shattering glass? I close my eyes -
and wait.

Picnic

We left two echoes in the tall wood,
Two staring faces in a still pool,
And whipped by thicket twigs, beset by bramble,
We sank our footprints in forgetful mud.

Labouring to the vantage point, progress slowed
By stony pathways, we traced the river's spiral,
And put names to every village in the vale,
As summer's drowsy fullness overflowed.

Then the busy fingers of an upstart breeze
Flustered the leaves and fired a pheasant's frenzy
To fly amok in colonnaded corn.

Our shadows merged on warm stone as memories
Set firm, and we made for the maddening city
All echoes dwindling, all reflections gone.

Cryptography

So what
if intellect
and poet's art
can neatly set
conceit and words
at loggerheads

so making sense
and reference
linger aloof
eureka-proof
in permanent
disfigurement?

but what
if intellect
and critic's craft
can so redraft
or reconstruct
to resurrect

a newer guise
of pure surmise?
In such a game
should we acclaim
a fraudulent
decipherment?

If I Were King Of Poetry

There'd be no moon
no golden June
the rose would go
and so would snow.

I'd banish birds
and pretty words
to honour sense
and even science

I'd order curbs
on woolly verbs
and work the sieves
on adjectives.

I'd tear apart
the throbbing heart,
expose the nerve
of beauty's curve

proclaim an age
of righteous rage
at passion spent
on sentiment.

But some would see
a tyranny
and no doubt brew
a palace coup,

urge the rabble
with fiery babble,
perhaps decide
a regicide.

Then back would come
the beating drum
the blood-red rose
and endless snows.
Not quite perhaps
a full eclipse
but tempered now
with knowledge how

to see again
with acumen.
If so my reign
would not have been
too much in vain

had I been king of poetry.

Poetry Workshop

The wordsmiths are hard at work today—
Banging away at similes, knocking stanzas
Into shape, and jointing clever rhyme schemes.
The foreman, a true craftsman, assists
In setting out some intricate free verse.
He looks pleased—indeed he should—
So early in the day and ten lines of an epic ode,
Two ballads and a near-completed sonnet on death.
Already the floor is deep in waste
Words everywhere . . . .words, words, words.

Down To Earth

Down to earth
from a dream to a crump
with a jump and a bump
and a roly-poly forwards
quick peep upwards
to a pennyworth of sky
where dreams flutters high.

Lines To A Critic

Born to judge more than you can ever do,
You pull apart, dismember and misconstrue,
Your zealous disquisitions swept along
By the pure joy of finding something wrong.

Indoors

Snow lies
    Rain pours
Sun fries
    Wind roars
Best place

Indoors.

Word Magic

Words can kill us
we sometimes think,
but can resurrect us
in elixirs of ink.

Half Truths

If every truth is only partly true
And most deceptions only partly sham
What hope is there of chancing on a clue
To guide the wholesome doubter that I am.

Dissident

They went at first to clarify their terms
  hoping for an easy outcome.
He said he would reserve his judgment.

Flowers massed in the borders; unemployment rose.

They put to him compelling reasons for their case,
  entreating him to understand.
He told them he would have to think it over.

People strolled in sunlit squares; market traders did well.

Then some came with flattery and blandishments,
  urging a change of mind.
Not for one moment fooled, he simply nodded.

An onion sun hung behind the spire; inflation peaked

They sent in doctors,
  expressing concern for his welfare.
But he knew all to well that his fitness was not in doubt.

Freak gales flattened the wheat; a girl was stabbed in a city park.

A succession of psychiatrists followed,
  curious at his form of madness.
But he knew enough to dodge their questions.

Cold rain trickled in gutters; police divers searched a canal.

They begged him to reconsider, to think of his family
  and the harm he was doing.
He knew what they were up to, but stayed silent.

Early frosts scratched window panes; a minister resigned.

They made insinuations, hidden threats,
    doing their utmost to unnerve him.
But it made his resistance all the stronger.

As the nights drew in there was talk of a fuel crisis.
They teased him, tortured him, and mocked him
    waiting for him to break.
Now more than ever he knew he must not weaken.

They put him in an unlit cell,
    saying no one would remember him.
He told them to go to hell.

So they banged the door and left him
in a dripping silence,

where darkness was his only balm.

Fall Guy

They gave him this job to do,
saying he was the only one,
and he, eager to make a mark,
to write his name in their favours,
accepted.

They told him precisely what they wanted
and, sensing his eagerness to make a mark,
stressed how difficult the task,
how pressing the need for early results;
and he, perhaps more than they,
understood.

They said they would give him a free hand
but knowing how difficult the task,
how pressing the need for early results,
promised that every resource would be made available.
He had no doubt of what was needed
and knew they relied on him
utterly.

He worked long and hard,
mastering every detail,
and though the task was difficult,
much more than he had imagined,
he was spurred on by the need for early results.
Having a free hand gave him confidence,
making him willing to forego former freedoms
entirely.

The task gave him a new sense of importance;
his advice was constantly sought,
his progress reports keenly awaited.
He was clearly making a mark

and this more than made up
for the loss of his former freedoms
totally.

But difficulties arose,
setbacks that could not have been foreseen,
calling for more resources,
more time spent on research.
and though he was still in complete control
his sense of importance
diminished.

The setbacks continued,
bringing sharply into focus
how difficult the task
how slender the chances of early results,
how great the need for even more resources.
Recent findings, too, gave him cause to fear
that a successful outcome might not be
possible.

They began to lose faith in him;
his advice was no longer sought;
his reports were skimmed and discarded.
They queried too his use of resources,
making it quite clear to him
that the setbacks were his concern
exclusively.

He tried to make them understand
but his attempts at explanation merely annoyed them,
and in any case were too complex -
and he was the only one who understood.
They treated all his reasons as excuses
and busied themselves with other things
contemptuously.

Although he had striven hard
to do what they wanted,
to make his mark,
and write his name in their favours,
had mastered every detail,
exercised great care with all resources,
they were set on holding him to account
for everything that signalled inevitable
failure.

So those who had given him this job to do,
who had made it quite clear what they wanted,
had stressed how difficult the task,
how pressing the need for early results,
and who clearly, much more than he,
understood...

...deleted him.

Table of Contents

www.ingramcontent.com/pod-product-compliance
Lightning Source LLC
Chambersburg PA
CBHW071818020426
42331CB00007B/1523